BRIGHTON
Remembered
A century in pictures from the archives of The Argus

BRIGHTON
Remembered

A century in pictures from the archives of The Argus

The Argus

DB PUBLISHING

To order any of the photographs within this book,
please contact The Argus photographic department on:

01273 544614
or e-mail pictures@theargus.co.uk

First published in Great Britain in 2002 by The Breedon Books Publishing Company Limited
Breedon House, 3 The Parker Centre, Derby, DE21 4SZ.

Reprinted in Great Britain in 2011 by The Derby Books Publishing Company Limited, 3 The Parker Centre,
Derby, DE21 4SZ.

ISBN 978-1-85983-930-0

Printed and bound by Melita Press, Malta.

Contents

Introduction

THERE has been human life in Brighton and Hove for thousands of years, ever since Neolithic man and woman settled at a spot on what is now known as Whitehawk Hill. But the city as we know it now is a comparatively recent creation.

Not much of Brighton and Hove dates from before the 18th century. The Lanes, now a fashionable shopping area, was a small enclave of fishing cottages, huddled against each other to provide protection from the gales. High on the hill above the old village was St Nicholas, the mother church, which has survived until today.

It was Dr Richard Russell who made Brighton into a resort. He persuaded people to come to the coast and take the sea water cure, which often meant drinking it rather than bathing in it. But swimming in the sea was preferable for most visitors, who found the salty sea air was invigorating.

The Prince of Wales, known as Prinny, made Brighton fashionable a few years later when he came down to the seaside. He built the fabulous Royal Pavilion on a spot near the Old Steine and society flocked to the South Coast. Although bloated and selfish, the Prince could also be kind and generous. The debt Brighton owes him is considerable.

Brighton has had its ups and downs since then. One of the downs came when Prinny became King in 1820, for from that time he seldom visited Brighton, preferring Windsor. His successor, William IV, did not possess his charisma and Queen Victoria did not like Brighton at all.

She found the gawping crowds far too intrusive and retreated to other royal residences such as Osborne House on the Isle of Wight. She offered to sell the Pavilion to the town and fortunately this was accepted.

Brighton's next revival came when the railway was constructed from London and people could get there in an hour or two, rather than the best part of a day it took by stagecoach. Thousands flocked to the coast. They were not all that fashionable and the resort had to adapt to their needs but they were still welcome.

Other resorts began to take away trade towards the last years of the 19th century but then Brighton had another revival. The West Pier had already been built in 1866 but the construction of the Palace Pier at the dawn of the next century really brought in the trippers. At the same time, far-sighted businessmen such as Sir Harry Preston realised the resort's potential. He arranged to make the most of Brighton for early aviation and motoring while not neglecting literary talents such as Arnold Bennett, who wrote his novel *Clayhanger* in one of his hotels.

Another great man in Brighton's history was Sir Herbert Carden. He bought downland in danger of development and sold it to the council at cost price, thus ensuring the wonderful bare hills of the South Coast remain largely free from housing today. But not all Sir Herbert's ideas were good. He wanted most of the seafront and the Royal Pavilion to be demolished.

Brighton suffered during the two world wars with much damage, death and destruction. But after each one it recovered to be the leading resort for the fortnight-by-the-sea trade. In the 1960s it lost custom to resorts abroad such as Benidorm but had the savvy to be early into the conference and exhibition trade. It is still the top venue for chat in Britain.

The most recent and remarkable revival has been in the last decade. Just when it seemed Brighton might degenerate into a poor, seedy resort like too many other coastal towns in Britain, it reinvented itself. Now it is home to café culture, an arts-based economy and all sorts of other weird and wonderful enterprises. It is the country's capital of fun and frivolity.

There are great problems in the city as there have always been, including traffic congestion, poverty and a lack of affordable housing. But they are being tackled with vigour by councillors and business leaders who know the future prosperity of the resort depends on getting them right.

For the last 200 years, Hove has always been the posh partner of Brighton. It preferred to stay separate, maintaining that it was more exclusive than its neighbour to the east. But in 1997 the two towns became one and then the Queen granted them city status.

The marriage has done both sides good. Hove has become more exciting and enterprising. Brighton has benefited from some of Hove's pride in its appearance. Together they form one of the biggest and best coastal cities in the country.

Many pictures exist of Brighton and Hove over the last century and some go back

even further. *The Argus* archives contain thousands of them.

A selection of the best appears in this volume to give residents and visitors an idea of how much some aspects of the city have changed and how many others are surprisingly the same.

Adam Trimingham

Before 1900

The Steyne, Brighthelmston (now known as Brighton), in 1778.

Grand Avenue, Hove, in 1873.

J. Trusler's Windmill Inn, Dyke Road, Brighton, in 1875.

Brighton seafront in the 19th century.

An early Brighton seafront scene, showing West Street, Custom House, Sea House Hotel and Middle Street.

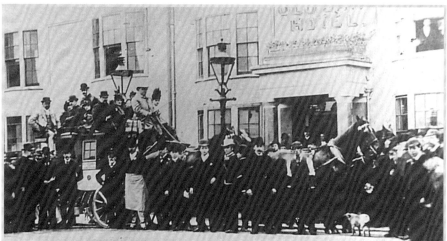

Outside the Old Ship Hotel, Brighton, in 1888. A coach made a centenary run on 13 July, 1988, following the old road and using the original staging posts. It arrived at the Old Ship at 6pm.

Ovingdean church and rectory in
1888.

Brighton promenade in 1890.

Brighton fishermen at Brighton Arches in the late 19th century.

The mayor of Brighton, James Ewart, leads the inaugural ceremony of striking the first pile to mark the beginning of the building of Brighton's Palace Pier on 7 November, 1891.

These two boys had just been sentenced to hard labour at Brighton in 1899.

The 19th-century face of Brighton Fire Brigade.

Brighton Chain Pier.

The 1900s

Preston Park railway station, Brighton, at the turn of the century. The station retained its Victorian look until the 1920s.

An art class at Varndean School for Boys, Brighton, in 1903. Founded in 1884, in 1975 it combined with Vandean Girls' School to form a co-educational establishment.

On 9 August, 1902, trees were planted in Brighton to commemorate the Coronation of Edward VII.

The entrance to the Royal Pavilion in Edwardian times.

The opening of New Hove Park in 1906.

Brighton Pier in 1900.

An eclectic group in
Preston Park in
Edwardian times – a
gardener, a man
pushing a bicycle, a
maid with her young
charge in a pram, a
man and wife with their
baby, and a little girl.

Jack Howarth, who
played for Brighton &
Hove Albion before
World War One.

Brighton & Hove Albion players at the start of the 1908-09 season.

The Royal Crescent Hotel, Brighton, in all its Edwardian splendour.

A horse and cart – but no driver – at Church Hill, Patcham, in 1900.

An example of early sports commercialism. Members of Brighton Swimming Club pose in front of an Oxo poster.

The original caption says, "A gallant rescue at Queen's Park, Brighton." It certainly drew a crowd but seems to have been less dramatic than the description suggests.

The latest conveyance for Brighton police in 1902 – a pony and trap.

Meat hangs outside a butcher's shop at the junction of Market Street with Brighton Place.

Egremont Place, Brighton, looking south.

The forecourt of Brighton railway station in the Edwardian era.

King's Road and promenade, Brighton, in the early 1900s.

The Palace Pier, Brighton, as it looked in September 1903.

Number please? Brighton telephone operators hard at work in 1905.

A large group of people have gathered outside the Pechell Arms in Market Street, Brighton. Captain Sir George Petchell was Liberal MP for Brighton from 1837 until his death in 1860.

The 1910s

Brighton Metropole Hotel, beach and promenade.

Another scene from Brighton Corporation telephone exchange, this time taken during World War One.

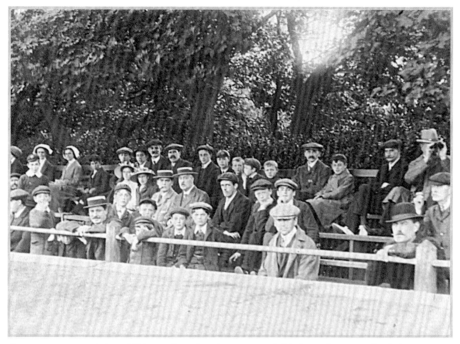

Spectators watching Albion play the Supporters' Club at Preston Park in 1912, but at what sport? Bowls perhaps?

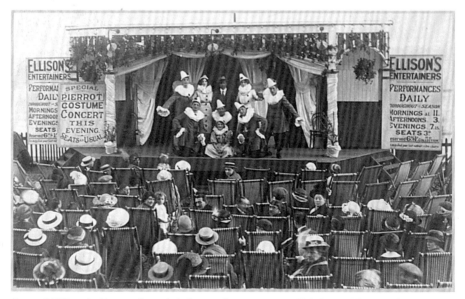

One of Ellison's Entertainers' daily performances at Brighton. The performers have stopped to have their photograph taken – and the audience has turned round to face the camera as well.

Our morning ride – these children have a ride with a goat along Brighton's Madeira Drive.

This group were photographed at Falmer Pond in June 1910. They include William Moolden, the Rev Bickertsteth and Walter Bentley (right). The child holding the pump was Gladys Green, later Woodruffe.

Part of the procession on Brighton seafront to mark the Coronation of George V in 1910.

Part of the crowd at the Brighton v Watford game at Hove in December 1919. Albion won this Southern League game 3-2. The following season both clubs were founder members of the new Third Division of the Football League.

The Brighton, Hove & Preston Dispensary in Sackville Road, Hove.

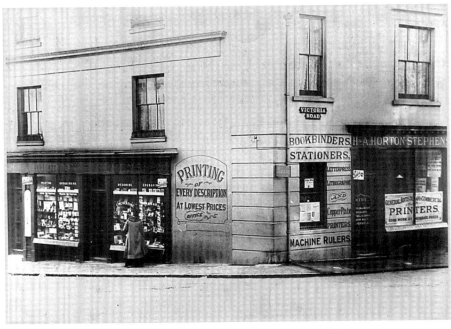

The printing offices of Horton Stephens in Victoria Road, Brighton.

New Steine, Brighton, as it was in 1918.

Victoria Gardens, Brighton, in 1915.

Black Rock, Brighton, showing a recent landslide.

Horse-drawn traffic only at Preston Village in the years before World War One.

A busy Brighton fish market, c.1912.

King George V and Queen Mary have just visited some wounded Indian soldiers who were convalescing at Brighton during World War One.

A languid pre-war scene at Preston Park.

The workers at Brooke & Sons monumental masons are all aboard a Southdown Motor Services charabanc, presumably ready for a day out.

The West Pier looking towards Regency Square.

Elm Grove in 1919 looking down to Lewes Road.

The Chain Pier at Brighton in the years leading up to World War One.

The 1920s

These boys were at school in Brighton in 1928.

Children from St Nicholas' School, Portslade, in 1928.

An almost deserted Hove Street, Hove, in the 1920s.

The Duke and Duchess of York – later King George VI and Queen Elizabeth – lay a foundation stone in Brighton in May 1928.

The Duke and Duchess of York pass through a naval guard of honour at the Pylons in May 1928.

Six hardy swimmers line up on Brighton beach.

Part of the crowd at the Brighton & Hove Albion v Norwich City game in the
Third Division South in 1921.

Shops and a pub in West Street, Brighton, in the 1920s.

The 1930s

In 1930 Needhams, of Castle Square, Brighton, were holding a closing down sale.

Haylons Cottages, more examples of Brighton's slums between the wars.

Haylons Row - demolished in 1933.

Pre-war Brighton slums in North Street.

Staff at Marks and Spencer's Western Road store in Brighton, during August 1936.

Once again there is hardly any traffic to be seen. This is North Road, Brighton, in the years between the wars.

Brighton beach 1938 –workmen are clearing shingle to put in putting greens.

The Ridgeway, Woodingdean, Brighton, looking north, c.1935.

The SS Brighton in West Street, Brighton, a busy thoroughfare in the 1930s.
The SS Brighton was the town's premier sporting venue, an ice rink that in
1957 saw the Tigers' magnificent victory over the Soviet national ice hockey
team. Built in the 1930s, on the site of the Old King's Head Tavern, it was
originally a swimming stadium which at the time housed the largest seawater
swimming pool in the world. Its name was changed to the Palladium in 1959
and it staged many big-name concerts. But after the 1965 Tory conference, it
was demolished. The new Top Rank complex, originally planned to cover the
site, was never extended that far. The space was used as a temporary car park
until the 1990s when the Oak Hotel rose up there.

Brighton Fire Brigade's Dennis limousine pump, being inspected by Chief Fire
Officer Birch in 1938.

Dennis pump escape belonging to Brighton Fire Brigade, in 1938.

Royal Engineers are called up at the Drill Hall, Queen's Square, Brighton, as war clouds gather.

Sandbags are piled around Brighton Town Hall in September 1939.

Digging trenches for ARP (air-raid precautions) at Downs School, Ditchling Road, Brighton, in the late summer of 1939.

The 1940s

Evacuees arriving in Brighton during World War Two, carrying their gas masks and other belongings.

Employees of the Brighton, Hove & Worthing Gas Company at the Middle Street department of the company attending a recruiting drive.

It is 8 May, 1945, and crowds gather outside Brighton Town Hall in Bartholomew's to hear the proclamation of victory in Europe – VE Day.

The entrance to the Palace Pier in more peaceful times.

Brighton Boys football
team on their way to a
match in the 1940s.

The Clock Tower,
Brighton, in the 1940s.

Brighton Corporation lifeguards in April 1948.

The Regent restaurant and dance hall.

The 1950s

Inmates at Lewes jail playing basketball in December 1959.

A street party in St Paul's Street, Brighton, celebrating the Coronation of Elizabeth II in June 1953. The young lad dressed as a drummer boy is David Brackpool, aged two.

An old tram shelter in Tivoli Crescent, Dyke Road, Brighton. It was proposed to dismantle this and replace it with a modern shelter.

Two young boys gaze into the water at the Level, a small area of parkland in central Brighton.

Brighton cleansing department sweep up on the promenade.

Each year tourism chiefs would select six women and transform them into Brighton Promettes. Their job was to sell Brighton to the world. They appeared in newsreels from Australia to Brazil and were as much a symbol of the town as the Royal Pavilion and the West Pier. In 1956 the *Evening Argus* described them as "walking information bureaux with sex appeal". These are Brighton Promettes from 1957. Right to left are Christine Bridger, Janet Selby , Diana Coote, Elizabeth Southgate and Judy Tickner.

The Undercliff Promenade, Brighton, looking east.

The 1960s

The County Oak pub, Hollingbury, in January 1960.

Holiday sunshine on Brighton beach in June 1962.

Easter Sunday, March 1961. Brighton people line the prom.

August Bank Holiday trippers at Brighton railway station in 1961.

Promettes getting into the holiday spirit in Brighton in May 1961. Their job was to help visitors with local information during summer weekends.

Three Brighton Promettes and three Ind Coope hostesses had plenty to talk about as they strolled around Brighton in September 1960.

Kemptown Railway Station in June, 1962.

Members of the Sussex Regiment march past the Royal Pavilion on 22 July, 1963.

New England House, Brighton, in October 1962.

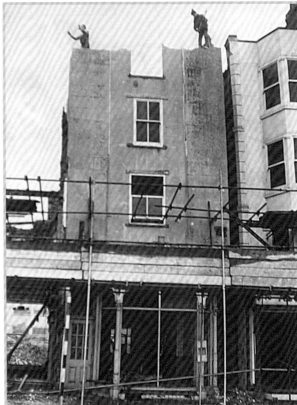

Demolition in progress on the Brighton seafront section of West Street in January 1963.

Sussex Heights, Brighton, in February 1969. At 300ft high it is the tallest residential building in Brighton.

Entrance to Hove cricket ground in August 1961.

Traffic travels under the bridge in Hollingdean Road, Brighton.

East Street, Brighton, in May 1960.

Hove traffic island November 1961.

Traffic congestion in central Brighton in October 1964.

The bottom of
Church Street,
Steine, in April 1961.

Brighton Clock Tower, Dyke Road, West Street, North Street and Queen's Road
in March 1961.

North Street, Brighton, in January 1960.

The distracting – to
motorists at least –
star on Brighton
seafront in July 1964.

Brighton seafront,
26 June, 1962.

Brighton seafront,
30 May, 1966.

Black Rock, Brighton, in the 1960s.

Black Rock, Brighton, under thick snow in the 1960s.

Duke's Mound, Brighton seafront, in 1962.

Brighton beach in the winter of 1962.

Collecting litter from Brighton beach in August 1962.

Nothing like a stroll before setting-to on the turkey. And the spring-like
weather on Christmas Day 1966 brought out the crowds at Brighton.

St Peter's Church, Brighton, in a midwinter scene in January 1964.

Skiing on a golf course? It was possible at Waterhall in December 1967.

A snowbound New England Road, Brighton, in December 1967.

Damage caused by gale-force winds and heavy seas to the Lower Esplanade, King's Road, Brighton, in November 1967.

The Meeting House antique shop in the Brighton Lanes in March 1965.

Window shopping in Meeting House Lane, Brighton, in November 1967.

Brighton Lanes, 30 November, 1967.

A youth gala in progress at the North Road swimming pool in July 1961.

An appeal for more help from lay members, including parents, was made by the new county commissioner of the Boy Scouts Association, Charles Mason, at the annual meeting of the Brighton district at the Royal Pavilion in May 1967.

Left to right are three local Scouts, Philip Wilford (17), Christopher Hammond (16) and Christopher Newman (18).

Armed with motor mowers, scythes, shears and billhooks, about a dozen members of the East Brighton Venture Scouts unit invaded Falmer churchyard for Operation Tidy Up in April 1969.

Winners of the Hove and Portslade District Scouts Football Cup. Standing, from left, are: 18-year-old manager George Steele, Jeffrey Roberts, Peter Wetherill, Robert Payne, Philip Combs, Anthony Peters, Derek Harvey (all aged 15) and 12-year-old Jimmy Scarratt. Seated: Peter Fairhurst (14), Leslie Trussler (15), Chris Robinson and 13-year-old Colin Steele.

These happy youngsters were among the Scouts taking part in the Brighton and District *Gang Show* at the Brighton Dome in November 1965.

Woodingdean Boys Club, Brighton, under construction in January 1966.

Brighton lifeguards in August 1961.

Andrea Osbourn – "I thought I'd had it!" – pictured with one of her rescuers, lifeguard George Wheeler, who said: "She had taken a terrific pounding." Andrea was rescued on 21 August, 1963.

Brian Hogbin and Peter Arey, two Brighton lifeguards who saved the life of a bather in July 1964.

Brighton Corporation lifeguards with their boat in May 1964.

Brighton lifeguards in August 1965.

On 24 August, 1967, Saltdean lifeguard Nick Rubens went spearfishing in his lunch hour and returned to the beach with this 22lb turbot. "The water was crystal clear," said Nick. Indeed, it was clear enough for him to be able to dive down 20ft to bag the turbot.

Children of Polish emigres at Middle Street School, Brighton, in February 1967.

The delivery man brings the school dinners for the children's lunch at a Brighton school in February 1962.

Brighton schoolchildren queue for their school dinners.

These boys wait to be served with school dinners.

Tucking in – those school dinners appear to be quite palatable.

Go on – try some. It's not so bad!

Young Brighton & Hove Albion supporters in February 1967.

Baseball at Brighton
Festival in April 1967.

A deserted Brighton
seafront on 15 April,
1963.

A group of girls from Roedean School in October 1964.

In the 1960s there were 100,000 books at Brighton reference library, containing every kind of information for local subscribers and here being checked over by three of the assistants.

Prisoners at Lewes jail
receive a talk from a
warder in October 1960.

Scrubbing a cell floor at
Lewes jail, under the
watchful eye of a
warder, in October 1960.

PC K. Thomas, of Brighton police, with Kim, the force's 10-year-old horse, in May 1962.

Brighton's new £700,000 police station is under way in May 1963.

Stacked in a top-floor storeroom at Brighton police headquarters in November 1967 were 300 problem white hats. With the merging of Brighton police with the other four forces in the county, the traditional white summer helmets ceased to be a feature of the town. The helmets were offered to the Gibraltar police force but they turned them down. This picture shows Herbert Holcombe, a storeman at Brighton police station.

Squatter families and their children crowd into the offices of the Brighton Welfare Service on the morning of 7 November, 1969, to demand accommodation if they are evicted from Wykeham Terrace the following week.

The last remaining building of the old Goldstone Farm in Hove in June 1968. The Goldstone barn is in Newtown Road.

A crowd of 1,850 children pack the Dome at Brighton for an afternoon of music by the Bournemouth Symphony Orchestra in July 1969.

In June 1967 this £50,000 restaurant opened at Brighton beauty spot Devil's Dyke.

The Brighton coast road on 8 January, 1969.

The Clock Tower,
Brighton, in
September 1969.

The 66-year-old Brighton Hippodrome came to life again on 10 July, 1969, with a preview of its new life as a Mecca social club and bingo casino.

The 1970s

East Street, Brighton, looking towards the sea in October 1970.

Blatchington Road, Hove, in April 1971.

The Clock Tower, North Street, Brighton, in March 1975.

Press photographers seem more interested in the crowd at Brighton & Hove Albion in November 1973. Actually, Brian Clough had just come to manage the club.

St Nicolas' Church, Brighton, in January 1976.

Anita Roddick, of the Body Shop, at Brighton in August 1978,

Mods on Brighton beach in May 1979.

Part of the Royal Sussex County Hospital at Brighton in September 1979.

An aerial view of Woodingdean in June 1972. The beginning of Warren Road is on the right of the picture.

Andrew Bowden, Conservative MP for Brighton Kemptown, meets striking Brighton firemen in December 1977.

The bottom of Moulsecoomb Way – the site for the new Moulsecoomb Leisure Centre – in March 1970.

Aerial view of the new Royal Sussex County Hospital block, Brighton, in June 1972.

The Royal Sussex County Hospital's pathology department in September 1979.

Christmas decorations around the Clock Tower in December 1979.

Kingswood flats, Brighton, in June 1978.

In December 1979 the mums of Moulsecoomb enlisted a seasonal recruit in their campaign for a controlled zebra crossing in Hodshrove Road. Children on their way to school were asked by Santa to write protest letters to East Sussex County Council putting the case for the retention of a lollipop lady. Since every child who wrote was to be given a sweet, the mums were hoping for some 300 letters.

More action: The battling mums of Moulsecoomb campaign for a controlled zebra crossing in Hodshrove Road.

The Greyhound pub, Pool Valley, Brighton, in May 1978.

Elm Grove, Brighton, in late April 1975.

An attractive addition to the speed trials in Madeira Drive, Brighton, in September 1973.

The mayor of Brighton, Councillor George Lucraft, presents the trophy to B. Rose for the fastest time in the speed trials at Brighton in September 1973.

Just in case. These vintage fire engines were on hand in Madeira Drive in 1975.

The *Brighton Belle* train on 7 September, 1977.

Brighton railway station on
25 January, 1979, with a
railway employee in
reflective mood.

Action from Brighton & Hove Albion's 2-1
home win over Blackpool on 29 April, 1978.
That season the Seagulls finished fourth in the
old Second Division, missing promotion to the
top flight only on goal difference after
finishing level on points with third-placed
Tottenham Hotspur. Promotion was delayed by
only 12 months, however.

The 1980s

In October 1984 the IRA exploded a bomb at the Grand Hotel, Brighton, where the Conservative Party leadership was assembled for the Tory conference.

Guests leaving the Grand Hotel, Brighton, in the aftermath of the IRA bomb in

The devastation at The Grand Hotel in the wake of the IRA bombing.

Firemen on watch at Brighton fire station. They attended the bombing of the Grand Hotel.

This is the problem... St Peter's Church, Brighton, in the summer of 1983. The warping though is solely that of the camera lens.

James Berney gets to work on the roof of St Peter's Church in May 1988.

Excavations at St Peter's Church, in July 1987.

A relaxed springtime scene outside a Brighton cafe in April 1987.

It was unseasonably warm at Brighton in April 1984 and of course that brought out the crowds.

Bathers enjoy the water at Brighton in the 1980s.

Rather less surprisingly, in August 1984 it was warm enough to take your shirt off.

Damaged trees at the Royal Pavilion after the October 1987 Great Storm.

The bus stop at the front of the Pavilion after the Great Storm of October 1987.

Even these telephone boxes did not escape the Great Storm of 1987.

Storm damaged roofs at Sedgewick Road, Hollingbury, Brighton, after one of the fierce storms of the 1980s.

High seas at Brighton's Palace Pier in November 1984.

Hardy swimmers at snowbound Saltdean in January 1985.

Snowbound Brighton seafront at Duke's Mound in January 1985.

Clearing snow in Brighton Lanes in January 1987.

A murky winter day in Brighton during the 1980s.

On 12 January, 1987, a traffic jam on the snowbound A259 coast road tailed back seven miles, as far as Newhaven.

A snowy North Street, Brighton, in January 1987.

A crisp snowy scene on Brighton seafront in January 1987.

Brighton postman "Ben" Gunn on his rounds in a snowstorm in January 1987.

Looking from Ditchling Beacon in August 1982.

East Street, Brighton, in December 1982.

He's got a lovely bunch – Ernie Winton at his banana stall in Upper Gardner
Street, Brighton, in March 1980.

Upper Gardner Street
Market, Brighton, in
March 1981.

Brighton Open Market
on a winter day in
1985.

The Cannon Cinema,
East Street, Brighton,
in May 1987.

Aerial view looking
east from Sussex
Heights penthouse in
November 1985.

Brighton seafront from
the air in April 1988.

A bird's-eye view of
Brighton in August
1988, showing the
Metropole Hotel and the
Grand Hotel.

An unusual view of Brighton Town Hall in 1989.

The dining area of Brighton Housing Trust in November 1984.

The Royal Sussex County
Hospital's new weapon
against cancer is
delivered in May 1984.

Part of the Royal Sussex
County Hospital in January
1983.

The depressing scene on the balcony of York Ward – the ward for Aids patients – of the Royal Sussex County Hospital in October 1986.

York Ward is demolished in March 1989.

Outpatients at the Royal Sussex County Hospital pathology department in January 1983.

Less than three years later... outpatients' clinic at the Royal Sussex County Hospital pathology department in November 1985.

Centenary appeal fund for the Royal Alexandra Children's Hospital, Brighton, in June 1984.

The Hare and Hounds pub, London Road, Brighton, in July 1984.

The Star and
Garter pub (later
known as Dr
Brighton's) in Pool
Valley in March
1983.

The South Coast
Road at
Peacehaven in
June 1985.

Brighton Corn Exchange in Church Street in February 1986.

A record-breaking attempt at the world's longest conga was part of the
Brighton Festival fun in May 1985.

The world's longest conga? Part of the Brighton Festival in May 1985.

The Festival fire-eater entertains the crowds at the Pavilion Gardens, Brighton, in May 1986.

Brian Horton, of Brighton & Hove Albion, shows these children a thing or two about football. Born in Hednesford in the West Midlands in 1949, Horton, a midfielder, made 232 League appearances for Port Vale before being transferred to Brighton in February 1976. He made another 217 League appearances for the Seagulls before moving on to Luton Town in August 1981 and ended his playing career with Hull City before going into management.

Brighton manager Jimmy Melia says cheerio to Albion fans as he boards the bus taking the team to London for the 1983 FA Cup semi-final game against Sheffield Wednesday at Arsenal's Highbury. The Seagulls won 2-1 to reach their first Wembley Final.

Brighton & Hove Albion fans outside the Goldstone Ground celebrating the fact their club has just reached its first FA Cup Final.

Young Albion fans are ready for the Seagulls' 1983 FA Cup Final appearance at Wembley. Brighton were beaten by Manchester United after a replay.

Brighton & Hove Albion fans at Wembley for the first match of the 1983 FA Cup Final.

A group of Seagulls fans who have arrived back from the first Wembley game, which Brighton and Manchester United drew 2-2.

The whole town seemed to turn out to greet Brighton & Hove Albion's players after the 1983 FA Cup Final.

A scuffle outside Hove railway station following a Brighton home game against Crystal Palace at Goldstone Road in September 1984.

Brighton & Hove Albion before the beginning of the 1984–85 season. The club finished that campaign sixth in the old Second Division.

Brighton fans before the start of the FA Cup fourth-round game against mighty Arsenal at the Goldstone Ground in January 1988. The Gunners won 2-1 and went on to reach the quarter-finals. Brighton, meanwhile, were promoted from the old Third Division after finishing runners-up to Sunderland.

Black Rock, Brighton in April 1984.

CHARGES		
8am-7pm		
up to 1 hour	**25p**	Sundays,
·· 2 ··	**45p**	**25p** Bank Hols
·· 3 ··	**60p**	all day or
·· 4 ··	**75p**	part of-
·· 5 ··	**90p**	8am to 8am
·· 6 ··	**105p**	25p Overnight,
·· 7 ··	**120p**	or part of,
over 7 ··	**135p**	7pm to 8am

Standard Charge £6 Imposed if ticket instructions infringed

Attach ticket to inside of windscreen on arrival
If ticket machine is out of order
use machine on next floor

Car parking charges at Brighton in February 1983.

A bleak sight on a winter day – the Dome car park in January 1984.

In September 1982 this Brighton policeman oversees the towing-away of a car.

Rockers reunion – the Dome car park was crammed to its capacity with motorcycles in May 1987.

A group of Mods near the Concorde Bar, Aquarium, Brighton, in April 1982.

Police motorcyclists escort Mods from Black Rock to a disco in Dyke Road, Brighton, in August 1981.

Mods on Madeira Drive in August 1981.

Parking meters in
Brighton's Old
Steine, in
November 1988.

Marco Swalet
doesn't like the
smell in Churchill
Square's NCP car
park in August
1989.

Varndean Sixth Form College, Brighton, in August 1988.

The 44th Brighton Cub Scouts join in Red Nose Day for Comic Relief in
February 1988.

Take your partners... adult education ballroom dancing at the Stanley Deason School, Brighton.

Founder members of the legendary Zap Club toast their first anniversary in October 1985. From the left are Pat Butler, Dave Reeves, Neil Butler and Angie Goodchild. It is still a vibrant club in 2002.

The Zap Club, Brighton - how it was.

The Mecca Leisure Social Club at Brighton Hippodrome in August 1984.

The proud manager of the Mecca Bingo poses in the splendid interior of Brighton Hippodrome in August 1987.

Eyes down for a full house at Mecca Bingo in August 1989.

Dancing the night away at the Pink Coconut nightclub in West Street, Brighton.

Nigel and Helen Peacock pose behind their new food bar at the Downs Hotel, Woodingdean, in December 1986.

The early days of
computers for
schoolchildren –
Brighton Polytechnic
summer camp in 1983.

Children swimming at
Surrenden Pool,
Surrenden Road,
Brighton, in August
1984.

Hangleton Infants School line up for the camera in December 1985.

In the 1980s overcrowding was a problem at Balfour School, Balfour Road, Brighton.

Some 68 pupils of Blatchington Mill School set off to meet the Pope in October 1985.

Janet Brown is the lollipop lady in Hollingdean Road in December 1983.

Schoolchildren cross Wilson Avenue, Brighton, in October 1988. They wanted a controlled road crossing here.

Joan Wallington runs the Dorothy Stringer High School tuck shop in January 1989.

Frederick Lind cleans
a Brighton street in
August 1988

Protesters block the
seafront road opposite
the Metropole Hotel,
Brighton, in a peace
demo in May 1983.

Peace campaigners' graffiti at Brighton in April 1986.

A Gay Rights "Section 28" demo at Hove Town Hall in May 1989.

Squatters took over a Brighton flat in Ashton Rise in February 1985.

Brighton squatters with a poster which reads: "Legal warning. This property has been occupied by squatters not trespassers. We are in possession and we intend to stay here. If you try to evict us with force we will prosecute you. You must deal with us through the courts contrary to the Act of 1381. By order!" The picture was taken in February 1985.

Anti-Nazi demonstrators take a short cut across the grounds of St Peter's
Church, Brighton, during a National Front march in November 1981.

An anti-Nazi demonstrator is pulled away during a National Front march at
Brighton Level in September 1984.

A demonstration against the Poll Tax at the Level.

Members of the union which represents workers at GCHQ (the government's communications headquarters) at Brighton Clock Tower in November 1988.

Brighton Aquarium and Dolphinarium in August 1989.

Brighton celebrates the centenary in 1983 of the oldest electric railway. Volk's Railway at Brighton was the first electric railway to provide a regular service in Britain when it opened to the public on 4 August, 1883.

John Ford, the conductor on a Brighton and Hove bus, in January 1987.

A new hotel and civic offices being built on Brighton seafront in October 1989.

Shoppers queuing at the new Sainsbury's in Brighton in April 1985.

Asda supermarket development at Hollingbury in May 1987.

Mrs Peek's cookie
shop at 10 Duke
Street, Brighton.

St Bartholomew's
Church, Brighton, in
May 1981.

St Bartholomew's Church, Brighton, is the centrepiece of this August 1984 picture.

Remembrance Day service at Old Steine in 1984.

Hanningtons store in North Street, Brighton, in November 1987. Brighton's oldest department store, Hanningtons closed its doors for the last time in July 2001 after 193 years' service.

Warren Road, Woodingdean, in November 1987.

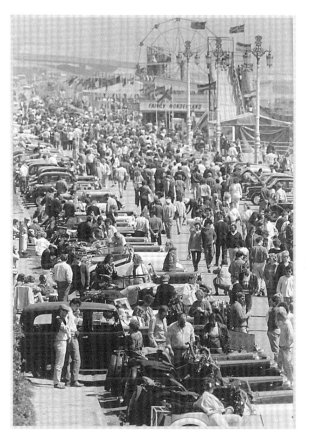

An MG rally at Brighton in May 1986.

Hopeful commuters inspect the departures board at Brighton railway station in June 1982 during a national rail strike.

These commuters are having better luck at Brighton railway station in May 1989.

Readers queue outside Argus House in North Road in September 1989 for free cinema tickets.

Workers busy sorting Christmas mail at the Brighton Corn Exchange sorting office in December 1980 and again in 1987.

There were few shoppers in Churchill Square on the day this photograph was taken.

Not so reverent – Queen Victoria's statue in Victoria Gardens was crowned with a traffic cone in March 1985.

Jack Smith gives Queen Victoria a good clean in Grand Avenue, Hove, in June 1987.

Nudes on Brighton's nudist beach with TV presenter Mike Scott (the only man in clothes) in June 1988.

Churchill Square, Brighton, in June 1989.

The 1990s

Boxer Chris Eubank marries his bride Karron at St Peter's Church on 23 December, 1990.

St Peter's Church floodlit in January 1990.

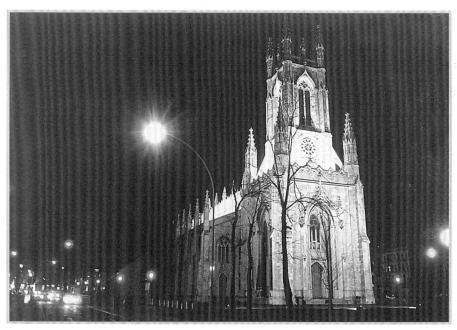

London Road, with St Peter's Church to the right, in October 1991.

Laurence Olivier's former house at 4 Royal Crescent, Brighton.

The Pepper Pot, Queen's Park Road, Brighton.

Winter storms swept pebbles from the beach on to the deck of the West Pier, Brighton, in 1990.

Brighton beach, full of sunshine in May 1990.

Angry seas at Brighton's Palace Pier in August 1992.

Brighton promenade
and beach is flooded in
August 1992.

Ice hockey at Falmer
Pond in February
1991.

Angry residents protest at a development of bungalows at Downs Valley Road, Woodingdean, Brighton, in September 1990.

Two boys ride past a boarded-up shop in High Street, Woodingdean, in 1991.

A new office building is "rebuilt" in Trafalgar Street, Brighton, in July 1992,

A burst water main caused problems on Brighton seafront in February 1993.

Police exhibit some of the fearsome weapons seized when trouble flared at Moulsecoomb in February 1992.

John Nuttall, site technician for Brighton Sealife Centre, in April 1992 with the newly-arrived tunnel sections for a new underwater walkway.

Young visitors at Brighton Sealife Centre get a close look at the starfish in March 1991.

The Pirates Deep children's play centre on Brighton seafront in August 1991.

The grim view underneath Brighton promenade in April 1990.

Traffic congestion at
Brighton Clock Tower in
February 1990.

Hanover Community
Centre, Southover
Street, Brighton, in
April 1991.

Pupils and staff of Brighton College leaving for Romania in July 1992.

Elm Grove Primary School, Brighton, in January 1992.

Patcham Infants School, Brighton, in January 1992.

Hangleton Junior School boys skip for joy in February 1992.

Madam Speaker... children take part in Hove School Council in September 1991.

Children at Blatchington Mill Business and Information Studies suite in November 1991.

The choir at Dorothy Stringer School celebrate being given the chance to sing at the London Palladium, performing in *Joseph and the Amazing Techicolor Dreamcoat* in July 1991.

Girls from Blatchington Mill School head out for a spot of rugby training in January 1992.

Agnes Baker, of George
Street, inspects this anti-
poll tax slogan.

Poll tax protest at Churchill
Square in June 1990.

Religious graffiti at Brighton beach in July 1992.

Fair play for Brighton, Hove and Sussex Sixth Form College. A demonstration at Pelham House, Lewes, in January 1992.

Pro-gay protesters at Brighton police station in November 1990.

Lesbian and gay pride procession in Brighton in 1992.

Anti-dolphinarium protesters in May 1990.

Churchill Square, Brighton, on a November day in 1990.

Two pigeons appear to be sharing a point of view in Churchill Square in June 1991.

What will those pigeons do now? Work has begun on demolishing the sculpture in Churchill Square in April 1992.

The new bandstand at Churchill Square in July 1992.

Philip Wrothy with a copy of the first *Argus*, which was found in a box of junk in January 1992. The newspaper was dated 30 March, 1880.

The A27 bypass at Falmer on an April day in 1992.

The then new Brighton bypass
north of Hangleton, with the old
Dyke railway line running across
the hill at the top. The picture was
taken in August 1991.

Belmont Street, Brighton, in June 1990.

East Street, Brighton, in October 1991.

There are plenty of cars parked at Jubilee Street, Brighton, in June 1990.

in June 1991 parking vouchers were introduced in Brighton. Here, Alan Dunston has one of the first flags for his shop.

Labour MP John Smith opens the East Wing of Brighton Centre in September 1991.

This little boy wasn't really getting a good telling-off from a Brighton bobby – but he is acting part well.

Oriana's disco (formerly Busbys) at the bottom of West Street, Brighton, in March 1990.

Brighton & Hove Albion fans queue at the Goldstone Ground for Wembley tickets in May 1991. The Seagulls lost 3-1 to Notts County in the Second Division Play-off Final.

The *Brighton Belle* train on 20 September, 1991. The engine is named for the *Brighton Evening Argus.*

Relaxing on Brighton's Palace Pier in August 1991.

In June 1992 June and Doug Sewell wanted to stop the pigeons frightening off flocks of customers at their Pavilion Gardens cafe. But locals were still happy to feed the birds.

Brighton's Palace Pier in July 1990.

Work is going on to refurbish the Pink Coconut in West Street, Brighton, in February 1992. Ten years later it was known as Club Barcelona.

In September 1991, Brighton boasted an official nudist beach.